God Answered
# LYDIA'S PRAYER

# God Answered LYDIA'S PRAYER

**LYDIA SACCOMANNO**

Tate Publishing & *Enterprises*

*God Answered Lydia's Prayer*
Copyright © 2011 by Lydia Saccomanno. All rights reserved.

No part of this publication may be reproduced, stored in a retrieval system or transmitted in any way by any means, electronic, mechanical, photocopy, recording or otherwise without the prior permission of the author except as provided by USA copyright law.

Scripture quotations are taken from the Holy Bible, King James Version, Cambridge, 1769. Used by permission. All rights reserved.

The opinions expressed by the author are not necessarily those of Tate Publishing, LLC.

Published by Tate Publishing & Enterprises, LLC
127 E. Trade Center Terrace | Mustang, Oklahoma 73064 USA
1.888.361.9473 | www.tatepublishing.com

Tate Publishing is committed to excellence in the publishing industry. The company reflects the philosophy established by the founders, based on Psalm 68:11,
*"The Lord gave the word and great was the company of those who published it."*

Book design copyright © 2011 by Tate Publishing, LLC. All rights reserved.
*Cover design by April Marciszewski*
*Interior design by Joel Uber*

Published in the United States of America

ISBN: 978-1-61777-755-4
1. Biography & Autobiography: Personal Memoirs
2. Biography & Autobiography: Religious
11.06.16

# Table of Contents

| | |
|---|---|
| Nursing Home | 7 |
| Childhood | 13 |
| Meeting Paul | 19 |
| Knowing Paul | 25 |
| Proposal | 31 |
| Paul Said No | 35 |
| Marriage Plans Underway | 39 |
| Marriage | 45 |
| Life Together | 49 |
| Boeing and the Birth of Kathi | 53 |
| Leaving Seattle and Pregnant Again | 61 |
| Toni and Her Misfortune | 65 |
| A Miracle of God | 71 |
| Toni's Operations, Then Priest River | 75 |
| Move to Spokane | 79 |
| Move to Seattle and Miracle Picture | 85 |
| George, Dust Bowl | 89 |
| Move to Long Beach | 93 |
| Paul's Misfortune | 97 |
| Desert Hot Springs | 105 |
| Desert Hot Springs Baptism | 115 |
| Sixty-Fourth Wedding Anniversary Revelation | 119 |

# Nursing Home

A rude awakening came when my dear, sweet, loving husband, Paul, became ill—again—and I noticed he was having difficulty relaxing and sleeping. Sometimes during the night, he would want to go outside to walk. I am sure this was because he was always thinking of me and he did not want to disturb my sleep. When I discovered this, I explained to him that if he went outside and accidentally fell while it was still dark, it would be difficult for me to find him. Then he would come to bed more relaxed and go to sleep.

On November 15, 2002, Paul went out for his usual early morning walk, and as he was coming to the backdoor of our home, his right knee gave way, and he fell to the floor. As soon as I had gotten him into the house, I asked him if he was all right. He said yes.

I called the doctor, and he strongly suggested I bring him to the emergency room in Palm Springs.

Oh, what a shock to think my precious sweetheart needed to be hospitalized. After Dr. Brian Williams carefully examined Paul, he informed me Paul had had a heart attack and should stay in the hospital awhile. I called all the family about Paul's problem; of course, they were all crushed too. Day after day, I kept praying Paul could be brought home and that he was fine. Oh, how I prayed.

The doctor kept examining Paul and finally, he said, "I think, Lydia, you should consider putting Paul into a nursing home."

I said, "Absolutely not… I'll take him home, and I will take care of him." Paul had other heart attacks and small strokes, but I could bring him home, thankfully. I knew I would do it.

When Paul was in the hospital for five days, the doctor decided he should be put into a nursing home. Dr. Williams explained this was too much for me, but oh, how I had prayed for his healing.

Finally, I gave up and notified my family of Paul's condition again. I knew this was going to be a tremendous trauma for Paul, as well as the rest of the family. Paul dearly loved his family, and they were his life, and the family truly honored and loved him. What a shock!

The time came for me to transport Paul to the nursing home from the hospital. The Manor Care Nursing Home was about twenty miles east of Palm Springs in Palm Desert, so I did not see a problem. Paul was seated in the front seat of the car, hugging his suitcase, happily saying, "I am going home. I am going home." He was so full of joy of that thought, while I was so bewildered and crushed as we started out for Palm Desert.

I think I must have been in shock when the nurse handed me a small piece of paper to give me the directions to go to Manor Care. I was too upset to ask for a detailed map.

When we started out for Manor Care, I was confident of transporting my beloved Paul, but Paul kept saying, "I am going home. I am going home." He said it so joyfully that I disregarded my small map and its faulty directions. We had gone down the road about five miles when I took a quick glance at the map.

"My God," I said, "I do not know where I am going. Lord, I need your help now." This was unreal!

I noticed a service station in the next block, so I decided I should go in and ask for help. When I showed the nice young lady attendant my small map, she nearly fainted. She said, "Dear Lord, there is no name, no address, and no telephone number! How in the world did they expect you to take your husband to Manor Care with this map?" I explained to her the hospital nurse gave me those directions.

She called the hospital and got the right person and gave me the full directions that I needed. I thanked her from the bottom of my heart and beyond measure because she was so helpful—I could not have found Manor Care without her help.

When we finally arrived at the nursing home, I explained to Paul he was going to get further testing done, which seemed to satisfy him. However, when I started to leave, he wanted to come home with me. Oh God, how tough it was for me to say, "No, my darling husband," and leave him there. I wanted to snatch him away and take him home. I was so crushed.

"Oh God, Please help me," I said. It was too much of a trauma for me to handle this alone without Paul and Him. Paul was my lifeline and still is. This was so hard to handle without Him. The devil had pulled another trick on us to keep us apart, but loudly, I said, "Greater is He that is in me than he that is in the world."

At this time, Paul and I had been married sixty years, so it was agony to leave him at the nursing home. Each time I visited him, he wanted to come home with me. I would have to give him one excuse after another, like having to go to the bathroom or getting a doctor's permission to take him home or getting a cup of coffee. I wanted to take him out for a ride or to take him to church, to lunch, but the nurses said this would be too great of a trauma for him. One day he had gotten out of Manor Care, and it took five people to get him back into the nursing home.

Paul had been my support, always my guide, my comfort, my love, and now to see my precious Paul in this condition just tore me apart. This went on for months and months. I could not stay away, and yet it was agony to see him like he was. Toni, our daughter, would come with me, going the fifty miles round trip every day. Then I had to cut back, going every other day, then every third day. I was getting so tired, weary, and worn out.

Now I am at home alone, tired, discouraged, and lonesome. Oh God, I miss Paul so much. Where can I find peace—the peace of God? Only in You, oh Lord, do I find the rest. But, oh, the hurt that I have to deal with. Tonight, with your help, I am going to backtrack into my youth that led me to this time of pain. Without You, oh Lord, I would have never made it, nor could I handle this.

I prayed, "So dear Lord, lead me through my young years so I can try to understand all this. Thank You for reminding me of the most important times in my life. You so abundantly provided for me, oh God! I thank You sincerely for what Paul and I have had and the good that is going to come out of this somehow. What Satan meant for harm, my precious Jesus is going to turn it around for our good. Satan was jealous of our love for one another and tried his best to separate us, but he cannot! But greater is He that is in me than he that is in the world!"

# Childhood

Only God could bring me through a childhood of fear; however, I have put yesterday into the hands of almighty God.

When Kathryn the Great ruled Russia, she wanted to exchange one hundred families from Russia to Germany and, in exchange, one hundred families from Germany to Russia to teach the Russians how to raise wheat. My ancestors were one of the families that went to Russia.

The Canadian Pacific Railroad sent representatives to Russia to bring workers to Canada to work for the company. The only stipulation was that they could leave Canada after working for the company for one year.

My father, Philip Kromm, and his family and relatives arrived in the spring of 1913 in Nova Scotia, Canada. Then in 1915, Dad and his family left Canada for Coeur

D'Alene, Idaho, in the United States and then later migrated to Whitman County in Washington State.

I was born to a family of farmers who were of Russian-German decent. My father and mother came over from Russia after my father had served his term in the Russian Army. He wanted to come to America because it was a peace-loving country, and he wanted America and its freedom. When my father and mother and older sister arrived in America, I heard my father say, "I never ever want to go back to Russia again," and so said the rest of our other family members who came from Russia. My father dearly loved his family, three brothers and three sisters, and he showed his love by his tender-loving manner.

When I was about four years old, I went out to take a little rest by lying down on the lawn, and, as I was gazing up into the beautiful sky, a sudden chill came over me, and I became frightened—so frightened I was almost frozen to the ground. I knew I was going to have the seizures my mother had; I just knew it. When my mother was a young girl, she was kicked in the head by a horse. She had the scars to prove this. She dearly loved horses and was around them until this tragedy struck her. Oh, the fear I felt, and I did not talk to anyone about it; I was too frightened, too ashamed, too scared.

In a few years, fear grasped me again as I was walking home alone when all of a sudden a man darted toward me. I was alone, and only God saved me from those hands trying to hold me and drag me to him.

Oh, how I rushed home, happy to be with my family where I was safe. Oh, how I thank You, God!

My father and mother dearly loved the Lord and our family. We spoke mostly German at home, and at school Mrs. Short taught us English. I loved school, and it became easy for me to learn.

My father received an offer to go to work in Colfax, Washington, where he could have a better paying job, a larger home, spacious yard, and all out in the country. It was a nice place, and there was a river nearby where we could go wading, fishing, and picnicking. Dad always showed his love for us by doing things for us. He loved to take us to Colfax, where there were parades, and the Fourth of July celebration was so exciting to all of us. We loved it for the excitement it held for us.

Then one day, when I was seven years old, tragedy struck. My father and younger brother, Robert, took off to go get some apples at the neighbor's farm. Coming back from the neighbor's, Dad's car just stopped directly on the railroad tracks. The neighbor told us later (they saw the accident) my father had gotten out of the car to see what the problem was. My father looked up, and there was the train upon them, and my father had a choice to make—either save himself or save my brother. My father chose to save my brother, so in a split second, he reached in the topless car and grabbed brother Robert and threw him out of the car. Robert received a broken leg and a cut on his head, but my precious father was killed instantly. The train had not blown its whistle as it came to the crossing. This happened August 15, 1927.

Oh, how we loved our dad, and this would have wiped out my mother had it not been for the Lord. My mother cried, "Oh Lord, now what do we do?"

Then Grandma Wagner showed up to "help" us, and, oh, how she took over. She was that kind of a person. She was stern and wanted to handle everything, money and all. We moved to Endicott, where we could be close to her and her dictates. My mother had no schooling, so she went along with what Grandma suggested sternly.

Oh God, thank You for helping us and helping to deal with Grandma's directions. We—all my brothers and sisters and mother—moved into a large two-room home. My older sister, Marie, had gotten married and was living in Endicott, so that made it nice for us to visit her and her family.

I was encouraged to go to church by my mother because she was depending on His help, and she kept praying for each of us to attend. It felt so good experiencing the love of God.

When I was in the sixth grade, Grandma said I should go out and earn some money for myself. *Good*, I thought, but after I had worked hard this one summer for a wheat farmer during the harvest time, putting in long hours, Grandma said I should give the money to her. I was hurt, but that was Grandma, and my mother just looked at me and shook her head in disgust.

When I was twelve years old, I had my first seizure, the one and only seizure for many years. This frightened me and, oh, how I depended on God to help to understand what was going on.

After I graduated from the eighth grade, my grandmother said I should seek other means for my education. Of course, I was crushed because I felt the seizure played a part in her decision, but I was only fourteen years old. Oh God, help!

I investigated, sought help from the church, and asked questions about what I should do. One day as I was out for a walk, my steps brought me to a nice-looking farmhouse on a side hill. I had heard Mrs. Rockwell, the owner of the farmhouse, helped people in need, so I stopped and introduced myself and told her I needed help; I would like to work my way through high school, if it was at all possible. The Rockwells were a nice family. Mr. and Mrs. Jay Rockwell had a son, Franklin, in the twelfth grade at Endicott High School.

Mrs. Rockwell said, "By all means, come a week before school starts, and we will work together." Oh God, what an angel she was; a stern but a loving, highly educated person—a Columbia University student in New York. I was so elated having my own bedroom, my own closet, and wonderful furnishings. She wanted me to have plenty of clothes and shoes for the winter. I only paid two dollars a week, board and room, but that was wonderful. I stayed with the Rockwells for four years during high school, participating in sports, singing, theater, and other activities. These opportunities may not have been possible without their loving support. The Rockwells were well educated, and their son, Franklin, went off to college when I entered my sophomore year of high school.

Oh God, what a beautiful thing You have done for me so I could get my education and glorify You!

# Meeting Paul

It was a joy to go to high school being so nicely dressed, having a good attitude toward life. This is a good world.

When I was about sixteen years old, I was listening to the radio as I was clearing off the dining room table. We had just finished a most delicious meal, as only Mrs. Rockwell could provide, when suddenly the softly playing music was interrupted by the announcer. He was interviewing what sounded to me like a young man from Priest River, Idaho, who had witnessed an airplane accident on the family farm. My ears perked because he had my attention, and I heard the most wonderful sounding voice I had ever heard in my life. His voice just touched my heart, and I said to the Lord, "God, I would love to meet this man." My heart was pounding wildly as his voice kept penetrating my thoughts for some time. I had heard other voices on the radio, but they did not affect me like the voice of this man I had just heard. Could it be possible to someday meet this man I had heard on the radio?

Gradually, thoughts of this strange voice began to fade, but I knew I was not going to forget his voice.

When I graduated from high school, my uncle Adam (my father's brother) suggested he take me to see a doctor in Spokane, where I could be examined for the seizure problem. The doctor gave me some medication to take to offset the seizures. Oh, how thankful I was. I was so eager to dispel my fears. Only God could do that! Thank You, Jesus! I am so thankful for medications.

Little did I realize the consequences of that request of God to meet this man I had heard on the radio. The scripture saying, "Ask and you shall be given," came to mind again and again. Thank You, precious Father, in Jesus's name!

It was a new exciting time to come to the big city of Spokane after being in a small town of three hundred people. The hustle and bustle of the big city brought excitement to me every day.

Uncle Adam had rented a room for me in a home of a nice family where I had my own room they provided. Also, the food they served was an extra bonus, and all seemed to go well, as well as smoothly. Uncle Adam and his girlfriend took me to dances, and, oh, how I loved to dance! The music was outstanding with a lot of rhythm.

Then after a time, I asked this family if they knew of a job I could apply for. They informed me the neighbor up the street had just quit a job working for a doctor in his home, taking care of four small children and keeping up their housecleaning. I would have to reside at the Spencer home. I applied for the job, and Mrs. Myrtle Spencer hired me on the spot. Oh, what a lovely home they had, Dr. and Mrs. William Spencer, so spacious, and the furnishings were beautiful.

Each Tuesday was my day off from work, and I would go to the bowling alley. I loved to bowl, and this was a way for me to get additional exercise. I met some nice people there, and after bowling we would go to a small nearby café for a snack. This was a nice out-of-the-way place where one could while away some time and just chat. The owner, Mrs. Hanson, had lost her husband to cancer and was anxious to sell the café. She sold the café to Frank Saccomanno. He was a truck driver near the bowling alley. He was a nice family man. He and his wife, Katy, expanded the café so they could serve beer and wine. They had a son, Joseph, and a daughter, Annabelle.

It was not long after when one Tuesday, I went into the café and noticed a nice young handsome man behind the counter. Our eyes met and he smiled. He came over to where I was sitting in the booth and introduced himself as Paul Saccomanno, brother of Frank, the owner. Paul's magnetizing touch of his hand in mine when he introduced himself to me made me feel special. He put his left hand over mine when we met while his eyes were smiling and looking deeply into my eyes. Those penetrating, beautiful brown eyes kept following me as I left the café with Louise Farnsworth, a waitress there.

The next Tuesday, I anxiously entered the café and seated myself in my usual booth with some of the other bowlers from the alley. It was not long before Paul came over to our table and sat down beside me. He then looked straight into my eyes, smiled, and put his arm around my shoulders and said, "Lydia is going to marry me." What a shock! I had seen him only the one other time before! To say I was speechless was putting it mildly. I know I smiled back at him, but for the life of me, I cannot remember what I said to him. I do not remember what I ate, as it shook me up so much. I did not know if he was teasing me or if he was serious. In my heart, though, I knew he was serious.

Louise and I would go out for walks after she got off shift, and before long, Paul and his buddy, Tony Rossi, would come by in Paul's Ford car, wanting to take us for a ride. We would politely say we needed the fresh air and the exercise.

I kept coming back to the little café each Tuesday, on my day off, not only for nourishment, but to see what this interesting young brown-eyed Italian had in mind for me. There was something about him that interested me very much. He was so sure of himself, so confident, and oh-so kind; my heart beat a little faster when he smiled at me in his shy way.

Paul's eyes kept smiling at me as I entered the café the next week, and he presented to me a beautiful flower. Oh God, I have never been treated so lovingly by anyone other than You, Lord. I know You are in control and in charge, and I thank You from the bottom of my heart!

# Knowing Paul

One day, Paul asked me if I would like to go to the Natatorium Park with him. It was located in the outskirts of Spokane, Washington. Excitement was assured because of the variety of rides, and they had a huge merry-go-round. Also, they had a shooting gallery. It sounded great!

We had a great day of fun and laughter, with plenty of snacks to enjoy. Paul particularly enjoyed the shooting gallery; his eyes just sparkled as he took aim at the target. His eyes were amused as I took aim and missed the target, but we both laughed heartily. It was such fun being with him!

Another Tuesday, Paul wanted to take me on a picnic somewhere close by in the area. The weather was perfect for an outing. When he picked me up at the Spencer home, he had a beautiful flower for me to enjoy. It was so thoughtful of him, and I loved it!

What a beautiful day it was as we started out in that gorgeous sunshine! We drove out in the country, where there was a lazy flowing river winding among the huge green trees. We found a huge overhanging tree that was just perfect for a picnic. Paul brought finger food snacks, and, oh, it tasted so good out there in the fresh air. Paul was so easy to talk to. The afternoon passed by so quickly before Paul had to go to work.

Tuesdays became important to me because Paul was planning to entertain me so we could become more important to one another. He wanted to take me to the Grand Coulee Dam about one hundred and fifty miles west of Spokane (one-way). I was concerned whether Paul could make the trip and get back in time to go to work." Happily, he said, "I am happy you are coming with me, and we will get back in time for me to go to work. We will be together, and there will be enough energy for me to go to work later. I am young and strong and full of vim and vitality."

So we started out on this beautiful day. The sun was shining brightly, so Paul rolled down the windows of the car. The fresh air was so exhilarating. How wonderful it was! Small talk of family, friends, and our work took up most of our trip to Grand Coulee Dam. The Spokane River joins the Columbia River at Lincoln, Washington, and then further west the Okanogan River joins the Columbia River at the Grand Coulee. What a breathtaking sight it was. The experience of this wonder of the world was something to behold! I shall never forget it and the wonderful day with Paul.

How I thanked him for being so kind to invite me to visit the dam with him, this most interesting place.

On our way home, Paul had planned another Tuesday trip: going to a movie at the Fox Theater, one of Spokane's more elegant theaters. Then he wanted to take me to the Davenport Hotel to enjoy a snack after the movie was over. My! His plans were keeping me busy…

When the next Tuesday came along, Paul gently and politely escorted me down the aisle of the Fox Theater, and we were seated in a good viewing area to best view the screen. The rose on my dress Paul had pinned on me had a wonderful fragrance, and again I thanked him. Paul lovingly looked into my eyes and smiled and said, "The rose looks good on you." When the movie began, our attention went to the screen. Then I had a strange feeling—a feeling that Paul had his attention not on the movie, but on me. I waited a long time, but I could not concentrate on the movie, so I turned my head to look at Paul, and he was intently looking at me, admiring me. Our eyes met, and he smiled at me. I returned the smile. Then he shyly moved his shoulder closer to me and put his hand over mine. My heart beat wildly. What was this about Paul that he could do this to me? After the movie, we went over to the Davenport Hotel for a snack, and it was oh-so good. There was a small doily under our place setting, and, for some reason, I asked Paul if I could take it home as a souvenir of the evening. He gave it to me, and it has been in my Bible for sixty-five years—the same Bible that Paul gave me four months before we got married.

"How would you like to learn to drive my car?" Paul asked.

I gulped. "I have never been behind the wheel of a car, but I will give it a try, hoping I will not disappoint you," I said.

He said, "You can never disappoint me."

"Then yes, I would like to drive your car." I wanted Paul to be proud of me.

So the next Tuesday, he invited me to sit behind the wheel of his car while my heart pounded with the knowledge Paul and his good teaching would give me good directions. I could do it. Paul seated himself next to me, encouraging me by saying, "You can do it." He started the engine for me and said, "Start out very slowly." We started to move slowly down a lonely side street, and when we got to the end of the block, Paul said, "Ease up on the gas pedal so you can get ready to make the turn." I did so. "Now make a wide left turn because we are at the end of the street." We needed to go back the same way we came, and when I had made this wide turn to the left, I noticed a fire hydrant ahead of me, and it was coming closer to me. Paul said, "Put your foot on the brake." He was so calm, but I got excited and put my foot on the gas pedal, hitting the fire hydrant with a jolt. The right front bumper connected with the fire hydrant, and, oh, how I was shocked beyond measure. Oh, how I apologized to Paul. But lovingly he said, "It is okay. This is your first time behind the wheel of the car." He comforted me and said not to worry because he could fix the bumper.

Then we both started to laugh. Oh, how good that felt to be taken lovingly into his arms. He was such a patient, loving, understanding person. Then Paul got behind the wheel of the car and backed it up. Then he went out to survey the damage. Amazingly, he fixed the bumper quickly. Oh, what a genius he was! What an experience that was!

I was beginning to learn more and more from that precious man, and I promised I would concentrate on the difference between the gas pedal and the brake! All with Your help, Jesus! Praise You, Jesus! Oh, how I thank and praise You, Jesus, for stepping in and helping us!

# Proposal

An evening of romance was in store for me when Paul invited me to a Saturday night dance at a large ballroom in Spokane. Each Saturday, this large dance was broadcast over the radio, and couples flocked to be entertained by the great dance bands. I had never been invited to go there before, so I was looking forward to going with Paul. I was delighted to accept his invitation. I did not know how good he was at dancing, but I had a hunch he could dance well. It sounded terrific! There was only one drawback; there was continuous dancing for half an hour when they paused for a commercial, and there was no time to change partners once the music began playing.

I was perfectly dressed for the occasion, hair was in perfect place, my high-heeled shoes felt ever-so comfortable for dancing, and I felt comfortable wearing perfume Paul would like. When Paul came to the

Spencer household to pick me up for the dance, he had a beautiful corsage for me to wear and lovingly looked into my eyes as he pinned the flowers on my dress. Everyone wished us a wonderful time going to the dance.

When we entered the huge ballroom, we noticed a large round sparkling ball turning in the middle of the dance floor, sending out romantic silver sparkling messages of love over the hall! How exciting too to see all those dancers on the floor having a wonderful time!

The reflections of the rotating ball made it so romantic, Paul led me gently out on the dance floor, smiling the whole time. The music was playing a catchy tune, putting me in a beautiful, romantic mood for dancing. I need not have worried about Paul's dancing—he was a perfect dancer, and I loved it! Paul had such a captivating personality that I had so admired about him! Paul danced so well that I had no problem following him in his leading. We danced and danced, loving every moment. The change in music did not slow him down one little bit.

Paul's arms held me ever-so tightly, and gradually I began to relax as he pulled my shoulders gently closer to him. My shoulders were feeling the gentle pressure of his arms pulling me against his chest. My heart began to melt for the love I was beginning to have for this wonderful man. I glanced up at Paul, and he smiled back at me. Then I relaxed and gently put my head against his cheek. He was always so polite and oh-so sure of himself, and I had the highest respect for him, and I knew he had that high respect for me. Oh God! Thank You! Thank You for Paul and his gentle spirit he has for me!

When the dance was over, Paul invited me to go for a snack with him before taking me back to the Spencer home. Paul was so full of love for me when he looked into my eyes and said, "There is a question I want to ask you before we get out of the car."

I said, "By all means, what is it you want to ask me?" He pulled out a small jewelry box from his pocket and opened it, revealing a beautiful ring.

He said, "I love you very much, and I would love to have you to be my wife!" Then he said, "Will you marry me?"

I looked up into Paul's beautiful, smiling eyes and said, "Yes, Paul, I would love to marry you. Tonight you have stolen my heart, and I have admired and respected you for a long time."

He kissed me ever-so tenderly, so gently, and oh-so lovingly, then said, "I thank you for becoming my wife. You are so dear to me." He placed his ring on my finger and then kissed the ring on my finger, sealing our love for one another. It was a beautiful ring, and it glistened in the dark. Oh, how I admired the ring he had placed on my finger so lovingly! I told him I loved it and I would be proud to wear it and become his wife!

Oh, precious Father, how I love You for giving me this wonderful man, Paul! I will cherish him forever! My heart is so full of love for You, Father. Thank You!

# Paul Said No

It came time for me to move from the Spencer home so I could be on my own and spend more time getting acquainted with Paul. I was getting tired and needing more rest, I guess. I could not burn the candle at both ends, so I thought I had better see the doctor so he could tell me what was going on with me and what the problem was. He examined me thoroughly and said, "I cannot find anything wrong with you; however, to be sure it is not the flu or something else that is going around, I am going to give you some medication to call a halt to this problem."

A few days later, I still was not feeling any better. In fact, I thought I should get some bed rest. I called Paul and told him of the situation. In my heart, I thought it was those dumb things we were eating for breakfast. We would meet at a little out-of-the-way café for a breakfast of cantaloupe and ice cream and giggle like a couple of kids. Paul was always telling me little jokes and stories to make me laugh.

Paul came over to my little apartment right away; he was so concerned about me. I decided I had better lie down for a while, so Paul brought a chair to my bed, where I was lying. He held me lovingly and kissed me, saying, "Everything is going to be all right. I love you very much."

All of a sudden, I had a seizure. I was not only sick but sick at heart thinking, *Now I have lost him, because who wants to be saddled with a wife with this horrible health problem?*

Paul was so concerned about me, and he assured me all was well. He would not leave my side for such a long time, stroking my forehead and kissing me and telling me again he loved me before he left. I was brokenhearted. "Oh God, how could this have happened? Oh God, I need You now, I need Your help," I prayed. I wept and wept.

The next day, I went to see the doctor about the seizure, and he told me, "It must have been the strong medications that caused the problem. You must be allergic to the medication."

Paul came to see me later that day, eager to check on me. I tried to level with him; I took off my engagement ring and tried to give it back to him. I said, "I love you too much, and I do not want you to be married to a woman with my health problem."

He was shocked and said, "No, absolutely not. I will not release you from your promise to marry me. I love you, and I cannot let you go out of my life. I want you to be my wife." He gave me back my engagement ring and said, "You are mine forever, no matter what."

Oh, how he hugged me as tightly as I hugged him, and I said, "Hold me, Paul; hold me."

Oh God! What a marvelous understanding man You sent into my life! Oh God, I loved Paul so much, I cried for joy! I kept hugging and kissing him, so relieved Paul still wanted me. What a tremendous release it was for me to know Paul loved me in spite of my health problems!

We hugged and kissed each other and, oh, the victory God gave me! This health problem had been such an unspeakable worry, and I did not know how to handle it, but God did!

Oh, how I praise and thank You, God, for sending this wonderful understanding man into my life to bring me joy and peace of mind! Hallelujah!

# Marriage Plans Underway

Almighty God, I am so thankful and grateful to You, even into eternity, for the love You have given me for Paul. Thank You for giving me a bright, happy future with Paul with special blessings and Your guiding protection that only You can provide. Paul is so precious to me! Thank You!

Paul invited me to visit and meet his family in Priest River. I thought to myself, *Where have I heard that before?* I immediately dismissed the thought. I was feeling a bit nervous as we started out on that beautiful day. I had on a lovely corsage Paul had given me, and I sent up a prayer of help to God to make me feel accepted by his family. They were so outgoing, so genuine, and they welcomed me wholeheartedly! They made me feel so welcome! Paul was a carbon copy of his father, and his mother was so receptive to me. Paul had always spoken so highly and so lovingly of his mother and father, so it was easy to love them.

Paul's father had come from Grimaldi, Italy. He became a US citizen on August 24, 1890, and he homesteaded many acres of land in the beautiful hill country of Priest River, Idaho. He was so proud of his family and his country and was content in their lives.

Paul announced to them, "We are planning on getting married." Paul's mother came over to me and tenderly kissed me, and I noticed tears in her eyes! Paul's father came over to shake our hands—how good it made me feel! I could tell Paul was special to them.

Paul's brother Ed was there, and he was happy for us, and, with much delight, he said to me, "When you are married and have children, they will have to be brought up as Catholics."

I, in my ignorance, said, "No, they will not." I did not know the teachings of the Catholic Church because I was raised as a Lutheran.

I asked Paul, and he said, "We will do what we decide." Oh, what a marvelous man he was for backing me.

Then I said, "Isn't your father a knowledgeable Bible reader?" I had heard Paul speak about this fact—he had served on juries in Sandpoint, Idaho, and also was a teacher in Africa after leaving Italy. So I felt if we could ask him about this matter, we could get a straight answer.

Paul's father said, "Do not worry. At this time, only in America, the Catholic Church is introducing new laws to be sure more Catholics would stay in the church—any other place in the world, this is not the case."

Paul was relieved and said, "We will do as we want to do."

I said, "Thank you, Paul, and thank You, Lord!

Then Paul's father said something that lifted my spirits to no end: "You do not have to be married in the Catholic Church, and you do not have to raise your children Catholic, and besides that you can be married right here on the farm with the minister of your choice! Oh God, what a miracle. Thank You, and what a great understanding man Paul's father was. Oh, how I thanked him for his advice and concern for us! I could tell Paul inherited his father's wisdom. I could feel the love they felt for me, as well as Paul, and for our future! Thank You, Jesus!

During a break from the wedding planning, Paul suggested we go outside and stretch our legs in the outdoor sunshine, so he took his .30-06 gun because he wanted me to try out my marksmanship. He took a couple of rocks and put them on a fence post, then handed me the gun and said, "Try out your ability to shoot." I took aim, like I had done this before, then I pulled the trigger, and behold, both of the stones were gone from the fence post! Paul looked at me in amazement and said, "Both stones are gone from the fence post." The gun had a tremendous kick, and the force of the gun drove my high heel shoes into the ground! Paul, again, looked at me in amazement, and then we both started to laugh. He said, "You hit the fence post and knocked both of the rocks off of it." Then he was instantly by my side to see if I was hurt and help me pull my heels out of the ground! We had such a good time and, oh, how I thanked God for Paul.

Then I looked around the farm, noticing a small creek lazily winding through the middle of the property. How wonderful was that trickling sound, giving off a feeling of relaxing completely. Nearby was a chicken coop where dozens of chickens were lazily roaming around pecking the ground. On the beautiful hillside were dozens of trees on the half-moon high hills reaching up to the sky. It was a wonderful sight to see. Paul saw me admiring the surroundings and said, "One day, I will take you up for a walk so you can see the beauty from the hills and see where the creek originates."

I said, "I would like that."

Further on to the left of the property was where Uncle Henry and Auntie Rose lived. Uncle Henry was Paul's mother's brother. On the way back to the house, Paul said, "Notice the oregano that my mother brought here from Italy." The aroma was so fragrant, and the looks of the plants were hearty and so beautiful to look at.

Later on in the afternoon, Paul went into the house to take back the .30-06 gun and, in a short time, was back with another gun—a shotgun. He said, "How would you like to kill a chicken for our dinner tonight?"

I said, "I will try," but my heart pounded wildly. Could I do it? I took a good aim this time because I wanted to please Paul. So, again, I took careful aim and pulled the trigger and hit the chicken's foot, and the chicken flew straight up in the air! I started to laugh; then I quickly handed the gun to Paul and said, "You finish the job." Oh, how we laughed as we fell into each other's arms!

Paul's mother cleaned and cooked the chicken for dinner and, oh, how good it tasted, for she cooked it perfectly! She was so sweet!

The next week, we drove through the beautiful wheat country to Endicott, Washington, where my family was living and where I grew up. My family was so smitten with Paul, and Paul immediately loved them. Paul had given my mother and family a huge box of candy, and they thanked him sincerely. My family made him very welcome—he had captivated them with his love and gentleness.

It was nice taking Paul on a tour of Endicott. I wanted him to see this little town where I grew up, where I went to my church—this church which held so many loving memories—where I went to school, and where I worked my way through high school—the Rockwell Place, which held so many loving memories of those precious people who helped me. I will always feel a deep gratitude of thanksgiving for them.

# Marriage

Our wedding plans were in full swing. Mrs. Spencer helped me pick out a beautiful wedding gown and a lovely veil—it made me feel special. I was so happy. Paul bought a handsome suit, and he was excited, counting the days for our wedding to take place!

Paul's brother Emery was his best man, and Mary Naccarato, Paul's cousin, was my maid of honor. My uncle Adam gave me away. Both of our brothers and sisters in our families were in the wedding party. Little Butch Spencer, about six years old, was Paul's ring bearer, and little Shirley Mauro, Paul's niece, was my flower girl.

My family arrived on June 7, 1941, for the wedding, and all were excited and happy for me. It was so good to see them all, but there was one huge problem: Paul's mother spoke mostly Italian, and my mother spoke mostly German. It was comical, though. Those two mothers were in a good mood and trying to greet each other while each of them was smiling and nodding!

Our Lutheran pastor, Olaf Eng, from Newport, Washington, came to marry us at an outdoor high-noon ceremony with all of the neighbors present; they came to wish us well!

A huge lunch was served after the ceremony—what a banquet that was! Pastor Eng offered a beautiful prayer for Paul and me and for the meal. I have never seen so much food at such a celebration, and it tasted ever so good.

Everyone was having such a good time and enjoying every moment! It was such an exciting day!

Then the music began playing, the neighborhood people brought their instruments, and they started playing lively tunes; the singing and laughter and dancing was joyfully flowing throughout the farm! They played special music for Paul and me! It was so enjoyable!

Before long, my family had to leave because they had to drive over two hundred miles to get back to Endicott. I hated to see them go but was thrilled they had come to share my wedding and to give us their wishes and blessings. Praise God!

Drinks were generously served, and everyone was enjoying the music, dancing, and each other's company.

Paul's sister-in-law, an Irish woman, was really beginning to feel her oats and then started a fight amongst the family. This did not set too well with Paul or me, so Paul said, "This is the time for us to get out of here." We said our good-byes, and we gave Paul's father and mother our deepest appreciation.

Our honeymoon began that night at a Priest River Hotel. Paul closed the door on the outside world to love and to cherish each other always. I was so proud to have Paul as my beloved husband, and I promised God I would love and cherish him always!

Oh God, how I love You for bringing Paul into my life to have and to hold until death do we part, for the best is yet to come! Hallelujah!

# Life Together

What a beautiful, wonderful world this is, having the LORD guiding our lives! Paul and I have the best life together with our love and happiness, living from day to day in the knowledge we are married for life and are happy about it! Paul was so proud to be my husband, and I, as his wife, adored him; never in my wildest imagination did I think this happiness could be mine!

We moved, temporarily, into a small two-room apartment close to where Paul worked at the café. It was quite an experience for us, as the bathroom was down the hall. Neither of us liked this, but it was to be only for a short time. It was common in those days to have the bathroom down the hall.

Paul always supported me in all that I wanted to do; he encouraged me with his love and devotion. I had quit my job at the Spencer home so I could be a full-time wife and take care of my precious husband,

and I wanted to be a good wife by being a good homemaker. He was so pleased to see me dressed in one of my favorite dresses when he came home from work. I also had my high-heeled shoes on and wore his favorite perfume that gave off a pleasing aroma, and I had my open arms to greet him.

I had made an exotic meal for him, and he was overjoyed at the meals I had prepared for him. He was oh-so appreciative of my cooking, as I have had a lot of experience fixing lovely meals while at the Rockwells. He thanked me, but I felt he deserved the best I could provide.

Paul, being a bartender, would bring me the humorous and comical happenings of the day. He was so easy to love! When the dinner was over, we would go out of the apartment for a long walk—a park was nearby—or we would visit our friends or just get into the car for a ride out into the countryside or visit the Spencer family.

My wish was his command, and I did everything I could to please him, to make him happy!

One morning, I woke up feeling a bit under the weather and sick to my stomach. I thought, *What is this*? I had my suspicions, though, and I mentioned it to Paul.

He shouted, "*Hooray*!" I mean, he was ecstatic with joy! He could hardly wait for me to be checked out by the doctor. Sure enough, I was pregnant! Paul's chest ballooned out because he was so proud he was going to be a father! Tears came into my eyes as he hugged and kissed me! He was so full of joy! Our life had a new meaning. He was so proud as he walked with me to get the exercise I needed so I could deliver a healthy baby with ease. The sunshine was inviting, and Paul was the stability I needed.

Oh, how he babied me! Paul would not let me mop the floors or do anything that was too strenuous because I was pregnant! I could not let this time pass without taking a picture of him with his chest so noticeably puffed out because he was going to be a father. I still have the picture today! Oh Lord, in my wildest dreams could I be so happy! Thank You, Father! Thank You! Only God could provide all this wonderful happiness to Paul and to me! Thank You!

# Boeing and the Birth of Kathi

A knock on the door of our little apartment one afternoon brought a new dimension into our lives. It was Mrs. Spencer. I visited with her awhile. Then because of our new discovery to have a baby, she rejoiced in our good success for a healthy happy baby! She congratulated us and wished us well.

"Now, Lydia, I have a favor to ask of you and Paul. I know you are happy at having your own lives, but now I need your help," she said.

"What is it we can do for you?" I asked.

She said, "My husband, the doctor, and I are getting a divorce, so I have decided I am going to move to Seattle, where I can go to the University of Washington to get my degree in nursing. I need your help by asking you to come to Seattle with me to take care of my children and to take care of my home. I have decided to rent a house near the campus so I don't have to use the car each day to go to school."

I said, "I think Paul and I should discuss this, but personally I would love to go to Seattle with you and help you in every way we can. You certainly have been a big help to me and a godsend."

I thought, *Oh God, maybe this is perfect and a blessing from God for Paul to enter a new career to get him out of bartending.* "What could Paul do to make a living while in Seattle?" I asked.

She suggested, "Boeing is always hiring people to go to work there."

With great joy, I said, "Hallelujah!"

When Paul came home from work, I enthusiastically asked him if he would like to go to Seattle. Paul happily raised those eyebrows, and with joy he said, "Yes, oh yes, I would love to go to Seattle to help the Spencer family."

I said, "Paul, you could apply for a job at Boeing. I know you like airplanes, and that would be a good experience for you. Before we were married, we went out to Felts Field in Spokane for an airplane ride. This is so exciting! What a blessing! Mrs. Spencer mentioned she would provide free board and room in exchange for me taking care of the children and keeping up the home." Hallelujah! This was perfect and a wonderful opportunity for advancement for him. We could not turn this down! We were so excited in this new beginning in Seattle.

Mid-August 1941, with our cars packed to the hilt, we started out for Seattle after saying tearful goodbyes to our families and friends. It was such a beautiful day as we began the several hundred miles to Seattle from Spokane through beautiful country, then up over the Cascade Mountains, then down into Seattle in the University District to 4717 19th Avenue NE—just one and a half blocks from the university campus! How exciting! "Oh, Lord!" I prayed. "Thank You for a new beginning for all of us in Seattle!"

We searched the newspapers for an advertisement from Boeing, and sure enough, there it was! Boeing wanted to train people to work for them! Paul was elated, and the next day, he went to the employment office to apply and was hired!

Paul had a new spring in his step. He loved his work at Boeing, and our future was not only more secured, but he was soon to be a father with a wife who adored him! Mrs. Spencer was so happy! We had such a great winter celebrating the holidays together and going to shows, parks, museums, and exploring the waterfront, where there were many fish cafés to visit and enjoy. The visit to the ships' canal area was interesting, and there was much to learn. There was so much to do in Seattle, with its mild weather, the laughter of the university students as they walked by excitedly chattering, the airplanes flying over the city, and the discovery of the University District. I found a gentle doctor, Dr. Donald Erickson. There was also a JC Penney store, movie theaters, and all kinds of stores only four blocks away! This was for great exercise, walking daily.

Then one day in February, Paul's brother Frank called to inform us he was bringing Paul's mother and father over to visit. This was a great surprise. They were excited to see us! When they left, Paul confronted me about his folks. He had a desire to go back to Priest River, Idaho, after the birth of our baby. His mother was not feeling too well, and he wanted to keep an eye on her.

I loved Paul. I guess I was being a bit selfish by having him so close to me in Seattle, but I wanted our happy life to continue. Having him so close to me in Seattle I guess I was a bit selfish, but I wanted our happy life to continue. My place was with Paul, though. The Spencer family was heartsick when we told them we were to leave Seattle shortly after the birth of our baby. "Not only have we become good friends, and I do so appreciate everything you have done for all of us and helping me, but we will miss you very much," she said. I told her and the family it was more difficult for me to leave, but I had no choice because I loved him and I was proud of him.

One morning, I mentioned to Paul we should get a supply of baby clothes, so we went to JC Penney for an eventful day of shopping I will never forget. We picked out some cute things, should it be a boy or girl. Then Paul said, "I need to go to the sports department a moment." In a short time, he was back with the tiniest, cutest roller skates, and grinning, he said, "We have to be prepared for either sex and their interests." How sweet that was! He had the biggest grin on his face and a sparkle in those precious brown eyes that made my heart go flip flop!

What a chuckle the Spencer family had when Paul showed them the skates! Who in this world would think about getting a pair of roller skates except Paul? Oh, how we rejoiced and cherished those skates!

Then one day soon after our shopping trip, I was feeling pain and started to time the pains, as the doctor suggested. I had asked Mrs. Spencer to check me out and then said, "I think it is time to go to the hospital to have the baby delivered." I left a message for Paul at Boeing, stating my condition, and I headed for the hospital.

When we arrived at the hospital, Mrs. Spencer checked me in. Soon, I had a tremendously hard pain, and I suggested to her that she should check me, and then she said, "I see the baby's head." She went flying down the hall, calling, "Nurse, nurse!"

In a moment, the nurse came in the room and gave me a shot, saying, "Normally this shot would kill you."

I thought, *What a thing to say to me now*!

She said, "We have to wait for the doctor to get here to deliver the baby."

The next thing I knew, the doctor awakened me and said smilingly, "Let's get this baby out. We have to hurry before the next pain." He said, after the delivery of the baby, "Paul certainly cannot deny this baby." (As if he would!) Oh, how I thanked the doctor for the delivery of our beautiful, healthy baby girl, and he said, "Don't thank me. You did all the work."

Oh, how I praise and thank God for my easy delivery. All those exercises and the long walks paid off! My mother had told me to be as active as possible so this would assure the easy delivery. Thanks to God and Mom!

When Paul arrived at the hospital to see me and our precious baby, he was hilarious beyond measure! Oh, how he thanked me and kissed me! He said, "I am a father, and you are a mother. Think of it. Now we have this beautiful baby girl who looks like me!" Oh, how happy he was, and he wanted to know how soon we could come home!

I know Paul dearly loved the Lord, and because of this, it strengthened his love and devotion to the almighty God! Paul was so excited, he said, "I have a beautiful family all because of the Lord for me!" He brought us home from the hospital, where the Spencers welcomed us wholeheartedly. The children cooed over the baby, as did Mrs. Spencer. Paul tenderly carried the baby up to our bedroom to the beautifully decorated bassinette and lovingly and oh-so tenderly put the baby into it!

The Spencer children loved coming into our bedroom to visit the baby or watch me bathe or feed her on the bottle. The doctor said I had enough milk for three babies, but in my youth, I had made my own bras. Because of this, I had underdeveloped nipples, so I could not nurse my baby, but she was easy to feed. The homemade bras were made too tight, I later learned, which may have caused the nipples to be underdeveloped.

Paul could hardly wait to get home to hug and kiss me and the baby. Oh-so tenderly and lovingly, he would pick her up! Oh, how he adored her! He would marvel over her features and say, "She is ours!"

We named her JoAnn Kathryn, after his father, Joe, and my mother, Kathryn, but we fondly called her Kathi. How proud they all were! Oh God! What joy we felt starting our life together with Your help and Your guidance and love.

# Leaving Seattle and Pregnant Again

Leaving Seattle with our precious Kathi was super. She was getting more beautiful every day. She was a good baby and oh-so easy to love!

One day, Paul said, "You know, we previously discussed leaving for Priest River, so do you think it is okay for us to leave soon?"

I said, "You are the first person in my life, and if you feel you must go, we will go." It was so much harder for me to leave Seattle because I had had Paul and Kathi all to myself away from outside pressures. I knew I was a bit selfish, but my newfound happiness had taken root into my life, and I was not sure of the future.

So after tearful good-byes to the Spencer family, who had been so good to us, we left Seattle. It was exciting to start a new life together with the three of us, but still, my heart was sad for leaving the Spencer family. My higher calling was with Paul and Kathi.

The trip was enjoyable, and when we got to Priest River, my, oh my! How they welcomed us! We received hugs and kisses galore, and the neighbors and relatives came to celebrate our homecoming! Paul's mother picked up Kathi and immediately turned her over to examine the crown of her head and said, "Your next child will be a girl." She could tell by the two crowns on the back of her head. That certainly was a new one for me. A single crown meant a boy.

Paul's brother Frank had a saw mill up at Priest Lake, Idaho, and also had a cabin if we wished to use it for a while. Paul said, "Yes, I would like to take my family up to Priest Lake for a while, but I think it would be better if we rented a small apartment or cabin where we can be by ourselves."

I said, "That would be great!" The summer at the lake was oh-so wonderful and relaxing, as we needed the time just to enjoy each other and the baby.

When we returned to Priest River from the lake, it was quite a change for us. Paul loved to work on cars; he could fix anything that broke down on the car. He was a marvel! While in Priest River, he went to see his long-time friend, Tony Jacketta, who had a garage and sold cars as well. Paul asked him for a job, and Tony hired him. Tony sold Chevrolet cars as well. Paul asked excitedly one day if it would be okay if we purchased a brand new Chevrolet car. I said, "Of course. We need a new car, as our own small coupe is a bit uncomfortable with all the things we have to carry along with us because the baby needs so much to transport back and forth."

Paul excitedly said one day, "Our brand new 1949 two-door Chevrolet is in the garage awaiting us to drive it out, and I want you to be the first to drive it out of the garage!" It was such an exciting day when we went to pick up our new car for fifteen hundred dollars! What a deal! It was so exciting to see Paul so proud to be its new owner; the car gave him a new lease on life! He was bursting with pride as I drove the car out of the garage!

One day, shortly after the arrival of our new car, I said, "I should go see the doctor to see if I am pregnant again!" How thrilled we were to think we were to have another baby again! Sure enough, I was pregnant!

Now this gave Paul an added responsibility. Paul had to find a higher-paying job, and, not finding one in Priest River, he was forced to go to Spokane to look for work. He decided he would stay with his sister Rose and her husband, Romeo Mauro. Of course, I was crushed at first, but he would get to come home on the weekends. He found a job at Boeing while I kept busy cleaning the house, inside and outside of the place. I got a few chuckles when I had painted the outside of the house, but at least I tried, and that pleased Paul's parents! There were streaks about every four feet, but it looked fine as I was painting.

"Father, In Jesus's name, how I thank You for giving me the love to do all I can to help Paul's mother and father, and I thank You for the love they have for me!" I prayed.

# Toni and Her Misfortune

I was about two and a half months pregnant when Paul's brother Stanley and his family from Kellogg, Idaho, decided to come to visit his mom and dad. That was nice, but there was one problem: they were exposed to the German Measles but apparently were not aware—they exposed me to the German Measles.

How tragic that turned out to be for all of us. What a trauma that was for me when I broke out in a severe rash. I had no telephone, no car, and a husband in Spokane, and I did not know what to do. I asked the family, Paul's relatives, and neighbors, and they did not know what the rash was. In a few days, the rash went away, and I was feeling my old self again.

All throughout the pregnancy, I felt there was something wrong. Paul took me to see a doctor in Spokane, and he said everything was just fine.

We bought a small house in Spokane so I could be close to Paul and, if necessary, see another doctor. The home we bought was a cozy three-room comfortable place to live; it was large enough for all our needs and close to a nice park where I could take Kathi each day to play. Her dad put up some swings in the backyard and fenced it in to keep Kathi from wandering away to play with the other children in the area she loved very much.

One day, I caught her in the bathroom standing on a stool and looking in the mirror. Her hair was sopping wet as she was combing her hair and crying. I said, "Honey, what are you doing?"

She said, "I want straight hair like all the other kids have."

"Oh, darling," I said as I was hugging and kissing her, "you are so fortunate to have beautiful curly hair like your dad has. We love you so much and are happy your hair is like your dad's." That seemed to satisfy her, and she loved her daddy, and if he had curly hair, this was just fine—she could have curly hair too.

Oh, how I prayed for the health of the baby I was carrying! Soon, as time went by, the upcoming event would be a blessing and my concerns would be over. Finally, on New Years Eve, pains began signaling me to get to the hospital. Sacred Heart Hospital was elated that I would possibly have the first birth of 1944 in Spokane at their hospital! Oh, the promises of gifts I would receive!

At that time, because I was busy having a baby, I could have cared less, but when the baby was born sixteen minutes after 12:00 a.m., January 1, 1944, I screamed, not from pain, but for the relief of an answer to my feeling of something being wrong. The birth was not difficult. Oh, the relief I was going to experience. The doctor informed me all was well with the baby. This made it worse for me. Was I losing my mind? I was so happy to leave the hospital, but before I left, a nun came and stood in front of me. Her eyes did not meet mine. She kept looking down at the floor, telling me my baby was not the first baby born in 1944. I was a bit hurt, but later I found out the baby of the woman who received all those prizes was born at 1:30 a.m. (How about that?)

We took Toni home under a shadow of depression. I thought I was about to lose my mind because I felt there was something wrong with Toni. I took her in to see the doctor, Dr. Condon, for her six-week checkup, and I brought Kathi as well. The doctor said both the girls were in good condition.

The visiting nurse came to the house to report further on the girls' health. She reported both girls were okay! I had bathed Toni earlier and had her lying on my bed. She was playing with her hands and kicking her feet—she loved to exercise her feet by twisting the balls of them in circles. The nurse noticed Toni there and asked if she could go in to see her. Of course, I said yes. She walked in and then almost instantly gasped. "My God, this child is blind." Imagine the horror, if you can! I gasped and ran into the bedroom, and she told me she noticed the cataracts on her eyes, and she said I should take her to an eye doctor.

I had been put through a mill—a run around, so to speak—when Dr. Condon did not have the guts to tell me the truth about Toni when she was born, or was he just stupid? I told the nurse of this situation, and she just shook her head and came over to comfort me by giving me a hug.

I was devastated with grief for my beloved Toni, and when Paul came home, he could hardly believe we had been put through this trauma. We fell into each other's arms, crying to comfort one another, heartsick about what our beloved little Toni was going to have to go through with her problems! It was unbelievable! "Oh God, oh how we need You and Your help and Your love and Your guidance and peace!" I prayed.

I felt like a curse was put on us for all the sorrow we had to go through. My prayers brought us to take Toni to a wonderful doctor, Dr. DeRoetth. He was such a loving, tender, caring doctor; it was comforting to talk to him, and he immediately gave us advice. Dr. DeRoetth had recently come from Europe and had the understanding of a saint. He encouraged me to play soft, loving music to comfort Toni, as she had been through a lot of trauma. He also looked at me and said, "You had German Measles when you were pregnant."

I said, "No, I don't believe so." I was home three days when I remembered the rash I had when I was two and a half months pregnant. My next visit to the doctor again, I mentioned this.

He said, "I knew it! It was recently discovered from Australia that German Measles can cause havoc to a woman in her early pregnancy." Oh, how I thanked him with tears in my eyes for clearing up this mystery, but I could not understand how this could happen to me. God must truly trust me to take care of this little angel who had this tremendous problem.

Dr. DeRoetth said, "In a few months, we have to mature those cataracts so I can remove them, but in order to do this, we will have to put drops in each eye every other day, but these drops are poison, and I am trusting in you and have faith in you that we can do this correctly. If you feel you cannot do this, you will have to bring her here into the office every other day so we can put the drops in her eyes."

I said, "I will do it, and I will do it correctly with God's help." It was a must I had to do for precious Toni and our family's well-being.

When the procedure began, Toni had a runny nose. This created another problem—stressful, to say the least. I had to be extremely careful, lest I made a mistake and put the eye medication into her nose. Only God! He kept me on track! *This is a testing*, I thought. *When will it ever end?*

To top off the daily routine, it got to where Paul completely disliked hearing of the day's happenings when he got home from work. Nothing but bad news on the home front! There were other family tragedies:

my brother Robert, who was in the marines, was killed on Saipan on June 20, 1944, and that was very difficult for my mother to handle; one day Kathi got into my medication; my brother Phil, who was in the army, broke his back when his ship left Australia, and it was blown up. He was miraculously saved by a life raft floating within arm's reach. I also lost weight severely. I said, "Oh God, please!"

When the time came for the operations to take place, Paul's mother asked her Catholic priest to come to our house and pray for Toni. Paul's brother Ed brought him to us, but he refused to pray for Toni, perhaps due to religious differences. I was so hurt, but then I said to myself, *Who in hell do you think you are to refuse a child prayer*? My pastor, Grosheph, had prayed for Toni several times. He had baptized her. I knew she was in God's hands. Paul was deeply hurt too.

Paul was so considerate of me, because he knew I needed to relax the night before the first operation on Toni, and he wanted to get a babysitter for the girls so he could take me out to the movie theater. Oh, what a thoughtful husband. Oh, this precious man had so much love and consideration to give me! Thank You, Jesus! From the bottom of my heart, I thank You sincerely!

# Miracle of God

Oh, how painful it was for us to take our little precious baby Toni to the doctor. She was to be operated on soon to remove the cataract from her right eye! It had been an exhausting six months in preparation for the surgery, so I was happy and relieved my part of putting the poison in Toni's eyes was over! What a relief that was! Thank You for clearing up her runny nose!

Oh Lord! How precious You are for all the help You gave me to administer this medication correctly, that You had faith in me and gave me the strength to do it! What an awesome responsibility You gave me. You gave me the courage to do the job You set out for me to do! I could not have done it without Your help! My precious, beloved husband had faith in me to administer medication for Toni, and the doctor had complete faith in me. Kathi would watch me as I put the drops into Toni's eyes. She watched as I carefully bathed and dressed her—she was extremely alert to what had to be done. Kathi was a blessing as she learned of Toni's inability to do things that she herself could do.

When both girls were dressed, I took them outside, put Toni in her stroller, and Kathi usually got on her swing. Later the neighbor girl, Bobbie Brown, would come outside, and the girls would chat with her for a few hours of relaxation.

On this day, Kathi came with us to visit Toni's doctor, which lasted only a short time, then we went home again so Kathi could go on the swings while Toni was put into her stroller and I busily fixed lunch. When Paul got home, the girls gave their dad a most welcome kiss. It was a long while before I called them in for lunch. Paul brought Toni into the house. Before long, after washing them up, we sat down at the table set for four and enjoyed light chatting—lighthearted things for us to forget the early morning's visit to the doctor's office.

After a short time, I put the girls down for a much needed nap while Paul, always so helpful in the kitchen, started to help me clear up the table and put the dishes into the sink. Before long, both he and I had everything cleaned up until the next time.

I kissed Paul before he went outside to do some of his chores, and I thought, *Now this is a good time for me to lie down and relax for a while on the davenport.* It was so good to lie down for a while to settle some of the earth-shaking problems. I must have dozed off for a while. Then before long, faintly I heard Paul coming through the backdoor into the kitchen. He spoke to me gently and asked me how I was doing.

That voice, where had I heard that voice before? A long, long time ago. Then I remembered! Dear God! I jumped up out of my deep thought and ran over to Paul, and I hugged him. Startled at my sudden actions, he said, "What is it?"

I answered, "Paul, it just occurred to me that I heard your voice a long time ago before we met! That wonderful voice of yours, I fell in love with your voice when I heard it!" Paul looked puzzled at my outburst, and then I said, "I have to find out something. Were you ever interviewed on the radio, years ago, when you witnessed an airplane accident that crashed on your property in Priest River, Idaho?"

He said, "Yes, why do you ask?"

"Oh, Paul," I said as I hugged him, "when I heard your wonderful voice on the radio, I fell in love with you and asked God if I could meet you. Oh God, how I praise and thank God for you. You are my miracle! A miracle of God has happened to us! Oh God, only God could do this."

Oh, how we rejoiced loving each other! When Paul realized I had asked God for him years ago, he marveled at the knowledge that God was so good and that He put us together! Oh God, how can we ever thank You and praise You enough for all the goodness and mercy You have given us? This blessing has never left us that we were meant for each other, but as of that moment, our life had more meaning, a new understanding, and a peace we never had known before.

Now I can understand the pounding of my heart when I first saw Paul, when those penetrating sparkling brown eyes smiled at me. Now I know You, Lord, are in control! Now I can also understand when Paul saw me the second time, he did not ask me to marry him then but told me and my friends, "Lydia is going to marry me." I should have guessed You were in control! Thank You. Paul has been an absolute blessing to me and our family from the beginning. The joys—oh God, I should have guessed. How I love You for putting my life together by putting love for Paul into my receptive heart!

I never did ask if the man in the airplane recuperated, nor the seriousness of the accident. I was too taken up by the moment, and then I forgot to ask Paul. Unbeknownst to the radio announcer, the airplane accident brought Paul's voice to the radio so I could hear it at such a time when I needed it most.

God is so good! God knows the end from the beginning! How we marvel of the love God has for each and every one of us!

# Toni's Operations, then Priest River

Father, in Jesus's name! How You helped us in the tremendous tasks to help our beloved Toni. Thank You. You prepared Paul and me to assist the doctor's advice and follow it to the letter!

Toni, at thirteen months, went in for eye surgery, and in a few days, she came home from the hospital. When we took her to have her bandages removed, we were so eager to hear the results. Toni could see better, praise the Lord! Then at sixteen months, the surgery on her left eye took place, but after a month, the pupil ran all over the iris. Oh, how disappointed we were. "Oh God! Help Toni!" I prayed.

Toni had a delicate body; every shot she got was a real trauma for her. Dr. Fischer, her pediatric doctor, said she was one in a million, and he then suggested we take Toni out of the city and away from people so she would not be infected by them.

We decided we should move to Priest River again; this way, Paul could keep an eye on his parents. To say his parents were overjoyed was putting it mildly.

We remodeled the upstairs into a large two-bedroom apartment with a large kitchen with lots of cupboards and a dining room and a nice living room with a stove to take off the chill at night. Precious Paul also built a small porch outside the double doors leading to the porch. It was ever-so relaxing to sit outdoors in the evenings, gazing out upon the Pend O'Reille River in the distance and enjoying the sunsets. The papered walls gave off a pleasing, peaceful, relaxing atmosphere. Then we purchased some lovely furniture! We did ourselves proud! When we got up in the morning, the first thing we heard was that creek flowing through the property—such a wondrous sound. Then we would go to our little breakfast nook for coffee. Paul, again, worked at the saw mill and part time with the Chevrolet garage.

The owner of the saw mill asked if Paul would like to drive a truck over to Prophetstown, Illinois, for him, and Paul asked if I could accompany him. He said it would be a beautiful vacation for me after all the stress I had been through (we had been through). Paul's mother and father took care of the girls, so it was great, and I was free to go. Oh, what a wonderful vacation it was for me just to relax, and I had to take care of the bookkeeping of the gas bills and any truck expenses. What a deal we had!

We had a marvelous time and had peace of mind knowing Kathi and Toni were well taken care of and we could enjoy the trip and scenery we had not seen before.

When we reached Prophetstown, we were driven to Chicago to meet the train to take us home to Priest River. We marveled at the huge buildings in Chicago and the hustle and bustle of those people just rushing around; it was interesting to see those sights. The train trip back was so relaxing, but we were looking forward to getting back to our precious daughters with the little trinkets we bought for them. We thanked Grandpa and Grandma, and they enjoyed the chocolates we brought them. They felt honored taking care of the girls, and they were no trouble. They enjoyed having them to themselves. Grandma was feeling much better, even though her legs were still giving her some problems.

---

Soon, it was time to get the much-needed diphtheria shots for Kathi and Toni. Kathi came through the shot just fine, but Toni had a terrible reaction to the shot. Her neck swelled up, and she had a fever of 104 degrees. I called the doctor in Spokane, and he said, "No doubt that will go away shortly." It did not. Finally, in desperation after a five-day fever, I called in a doctor from

Priest River; he came to see Toni but left because he did not know what to do.

Then I called the doctor in Spokane, and I said in desperation, "I am bringing her in to see you tomorrow morning."

He said, "You cannot because she will infect others."

I said, "I am bringing her in before the office hours tomorrow morning," and he finally said okay. We were in the office early the next morning, and he determined Toni had glandular fever, thyroid fever, and pneumonia. We stayed in Spokane for a month at Paul's brother's home. What a blessing that was! Slowly, Toni's problems went away so she could go back to Priest River, Idaho. My home seemed so good after all of that trauma we had to go through to bring Toni back to health.

When it was time to go to school, Kathi started in Priest River and excelled tremendously, but when it was time for Toni to go to school, the doctor said she would have to go to school elsewhere, as Priest River did not have teachers for non-sighted students. We chose to move to Spokane instead of Vancouver, Washington.

# Move to Spokane

It was time to investigate Spokane so we could find a home close by Bancroft School, and we found a nice home just a few blocks from it for sixty-five hundred dollars, which was a real bargain! Both girls could attend the same school; it was a real blessing to have a qualified teacher for Toni in this public school.

It was hard to leave the farm, where we enjoyed Grandpa and Grandma, playing pinochle with them and the neighbors and Uncle Henry and Aunt Rose, the homemade sausage, cheese, the huge garden, and the many kinds of apple trees—it was all a delight. On the farm, Paul could hunt for deer that was so delicious, especially the way Paul's mother cooked the meat. Paul was also an avid fisherman, which brought more of God's good food to the table. One day Grandpa told Kathi he was going to put some tobacco in her pocket, and sure enough, before long, a young deer came into the yard and put his nose into her pocket for the tobacco. Both Kathi and Toni laughed that the deer would do this.

Grandma and Grandpa were heartsick when we had to move from the farm, as they enjoyed the girls immensely, but we invited them to come to visit us often. There always was a place for them at our home!

I carefully packed everything, especially the valuables, such as the one and only picture of my dad that I should have copied. Sometimes, we put things off when we shouldn't.

So in 1950, we moved all our belongings and headed west to Spokane, Washington, but when we got as far as Diamond Lake, a huge wind whipped our belongings loose, blowing some things from our trailer. After we investigated when arriving in Spokane, I discovered that the one and only picture of my dad was indeed missing. I just could not believe it, as I had packed the picture in a secure place—in my jewelry box in the top drawer of our dresser, and I had put a towel in the drawer to hold it secure with all of my other belongings. My family gave me a lecture of my negligence to have copies made.

In Spokane, Kathi enrolled in the second grade and Toni into kindergarten, praise God, and Kathi's health was excellent, so that was a tremendous blessing. The girls missed the farm, especially the butter Grandma made and the walks Grandpa took them on.

On February 12, 1951, Grandpa passed away. He was seventy-six years old. This was such a blow to all of us, as he was the picture of health and he ate correctly. Ed was bringing Grandpa into Spokane so he could get a checkup by the doctor, and about forty miles east of Spokane, he had a heart attack and died (we found out later). Ed brought Grandpa over to our house, and I was the one who had to call everyone: the family, funeral parlor, the priest—what an awesome responsibility You gave me, Lord, and I did it for You to help out our precious grandpa and his family and Paul. Grandma came in to stay with us until the funeral was over. Then she stayed for a while with Lolly, Paul's older sister, who also lived in Spokane. She did not want to go back to the farm, for which I certainly could not blame her.

Toni had a habit of twirling in a circle. It was unbelievable how she could twirl in one place for such a long time. One time I timed her, and it was an hour and forty-five minutes of continuous twirling, and it was breathtaking to see her maybe slow down for a minute or so, then speed up and go super fast in one direction. When she got tired, she would lie down on the floor to recuperate, but she was always happy. I talked to the doctor about her dancing, and he told me no lessons but to let her do her own thing. I thought, *What a waste of talent.*

Kathi did her acrobatics with her feet flying through the house. I had to be careful, lest I would get in the way and interrupt her somersaults. It was fun to see those feet flying in happiness!

Again, it was time for Toni to have more eye surgeries. Calcium deposits were forming on the left eye, and those had to be removed. To top off the situation, we had no insurance to have this done in the hospital, so Dr. DeRoetth performed those surgeries in his office to save us money. What a doctor and a saint! I would go to the office with her so she would not be alone. My stomach was so nervous but, with God's help, I held steady as the doctor poked the long needle into her left eye. Oh God, what an awesome God You are to help us when we needed help so very much! Paul had to go to work, but he was also my support and comfort!

Kathi would stay with Annabelle while the surgery was going on. She was a tremendous help to us.

Toni graduated from Bancroft grade school in 1959 in Spokane. Her schooling consisted of a one-room class with all the eight grades of non-sighted students. Naturally, Mr. Toth, the teacher, did not have the time to spend with each student as needed. This was a tremendous handicap for Toni to endure.

Toni became faced with another problem—to go to school in Vancouver, Washington, the state school for the blind, four hundred miles from home. The doctor helped us get Toni enrolled there. Of course, this was another severe blow to Toni, Paul, Kathi, and me. Oh, how I had prayed for another solution, but to no avail. We were crushed to have to leave her there, but brave Toni took it like a trooper. We three—Paul, Kathi, and I—would drive to see her as often as we could, at least once a month. Toni was elated and proud to introduce us to her teachers.

Kathi kept us busy with her activities at North Central High School. Boyfriends flocked around her, as she was a charming young girl. She had charisma she inherited from her dad. While still in school, she took a course in bookkeeping, then after graduation, she went to work for Montgomery Ward. She was a wizard at figures. She enjoyed the work, and it became easy for her!

I started to have extra time on my hands. Paul was busy working all day, and in the evening sometimes, he helped out at the garage repairing cars, so I asked Paul if it would be okay with him if I went out to do some work to bring in some extra cash for the household. He said, "By all means, if this is what you want to do, that would be just fine with me, and we could use the extra money."

I applied at the Crescent Store, where I did some Christmas-package wrapping. It was a superstore, where they sold all sorts of things; I bought our first television set and bought many other extras we needed. Then I decided I wanted to do more work, so I asked my neighbor, Joe Stewart, who was the Spokane County Treasurer, if he could use me, as I was interested in extra work. He hired me, and I learned the office from the ground up, so to speak. It was interesting, and I took to it like a duck takes to water. It was not long before I was appointed the chief counter clerk of the treasurer's office of Spokane County by

Mr. Stewart. I was in charge of 175,000 pieces of mail, tax statements, payments from property owners, and other clerical duties pertaining to the busy front office. I loved the work, and it was a challenge to me.

After she left Montgomery Ward, Kathi went to work for B. F. Goodrich, where she met and fell in love with LeRoy Shaw. After a whirlwind romance, they decided to get married on August 15, 1965. She had a most beautiful wedding! The wedding took place in Emanuel Lutheran Church with about four hundred guests attending.

Shortly after Mr. Stewart passed away, I took a six-month leave of absence so I could accompany Paul to Rapid City, South Dakota, while the landing strip in Spokane was being repaired at Fairchild. It was a nice vacation for me to relax after a lot of stress I had been through and to spend valuable time with Paul. We both had to catch up and slow down! It was quite an event to visit Mt. Rushmore and explore the area with friends. We found a joyous, outgoing church and many activities to keep us busy.

All praise and thanks to God. Only His love do we raise our hearts to!

# Move to Seattle and Miracle Picture

When Paul, Toni, and I returned from Rapid City, South Dakota, Toni had another decision to make about her schooling. She had finished high school at Vancouver, Washington, and was being sent to Seattle to train for a job at the lighthouse for the blind. Paul thought if we went to Seattle, he could go to work at Boeing again, and, of course, I had to quit my job at the treasurer's office in order to do this. We left Spokane in the fall of 1965.

Kathi and LeRoy moved into our house. Kathi was pregnant with Lance, and he was born May 25, 1966. Later on, Vance was born July 23, 1969, and Casi on November 20, 1970.

Paul and I became apartment managers in Rainier Beach. This was quite a change, and it was surprising the rules we had to maintain.

I applied for work at the post office and worked holidays. Then I became very active in the Lutheran church and became the treasurer for the whole Seattle area. I was a busy girl. And I also took up public speaking. I tire just thinking how busy I was. Toni had moved in with us and took up organ playing as a hobby. She was doing very well. She had a problem making good connections on the bus for work, so Paul had an idea: let us build her a house within walking distance of her work. Yes, we found a nice vacant lot just a half block from the lighthouse for the blind. Then the work began. Oh, how busy we were. Lumbermen built the first home in the Seattle area for Toni. It was fun finishing her cute little home; it was a challenge, and there was much to do. Toni was so proud of her home.

Toni's home completed, I found time on my hands again. Across the street from our apartment, the school district was planning to build a junior high school. I applied for the job of operating the kitchen, the first ever for the satellite program. People came from all over the US and overseas to view the program. It was a new idea where meals similar to the meals on the airlines were served. To say it was different was putting it mildly.

Paul liked to nip on the bottle, and one Christmas—he loved his wine (growing up with it)—he had too much, and it created some soreness in his chest over time. My brother, a nurse anesthetist, recommended a good doctor for Paul to see in Spokane, so we went there for the surgery to correct the flow of urine.

After that, Kathi's husband got sick from cancer, and he was quite ill.

One weekend about this time, we decided to make a trip to Endicott to visit my family. It was such a nice treat to get away for a while. On our way back, we brought my sister Marie with us to visit awhile. It was quite an experience for her to get away too. She had been ill with TB for some time but became free of that disease.

We talked of many family issues, and the problem came up again about the family picture I had lost in 1950. She said it was too bad I had not made copies of the only picture of my dad. This hurt me to the core, though. Marie was family-oriented and was deeply concerned about such matters. She meant no harm, but my feelings were hurt. I stated, "I should have made extra copies, but I had not done so."

That night, I cried out to the Lord, saying, "In desperation, I am crying out to You, Lord. You know I did not lose that picture on purpose." And oh, how sorry I was, and I asked for forgiveness for being so shortsighted. I felt calmer after praying and finally went to sleep. Marie left in a few days, and then one day it happened! I had just purchased a new filing cabinet from Sears, and I opened the top drawer of the filing cabinet, and there was the lost picture! Oh, how I worshiped the Lord and praised Him for the picture—the picture that had been lost twenty-two years ago when we moved in from Priest River, Idaho, and here we were in Seattle twenty-two years later! Only God could have put this miracle picture in the filing cabinet. What a miracle for my family and me. Needless to say, I had copies made immediately and sent copies to all of my family! How relieved I was to do this for my family and that it was done only to give God all the glory! I have the original picture in my family Bible. My family responded with great joy, and their reactions were enormous!

When Kathi's husband passed away April 23, 1976, it was a trying time for Kathi and her family. Little Casi came to stay with us for a while. Then Paul decided he should retire so he could help out in any way he could, making life a bit easier for Kathi. By this time, Toni had gotten a dog, Pretzel, a wiener dog, to be with her, so we felt we could move over to George, Washington, to our little place halfway between Seattle and Spokane.

Oh, the grace and mercy of God let us to do the right things for our family and especially to bring glory to God in all things!

# George, Dust Bowl

Paul and I needed to get away from all of the responsibilities and activities, so we went out of town to George, Washington—halfway between Seattle and Spokane—and we bought a lot and a half and a nice two-room trailer—we were going to vacation! This was a great way to get away, so to speak, from the hustle and bustle of the city of Seattle. There was just one problem: Just across the street from our property was Washington's largest cherry orchard—sour cherry—where we encountered dust. Oh, how I hate dust! I had to dust several times a day and had to wash the plates before we could eat off them. Granted, it was spring when we moved in, so I thought it surely would let up before too many months. It did, some, but I had to carry my Kleenex box wherever I went. Dust did not bother Paul; he loved being out in the open.

The people of George were super, so happy, and carefree. We found some of the most fun-loving people there that I have ever seen. The church had a square-dance caller, so we learned to square and round dance. This was such fun. Paul sincerely was having a good time with these wonderful people and was comfortable living there.

Shortly after we moved to George, we met Wanda and Ike Needens and Helen and Al Lind—two of the most God-fearing couples in George. They all attended the same Lutheran church as Paul and I. The Linds would have us up their place every Fourth of July for a picnic in their yard with a lot of people from the church there too.

Wanda and Ike were still deeply religious—the most loving people; the Lord and their love just explodes from inside them. Their love shines from their hearts to all who will receive, and Paul and I did receive. I began to believe in the power of the Lord Jesus Christ and His healing power, which we confess each day!

Casi came to stay with us for a while; she was an absolute darling to have with us, so energetic and helpful. She enjoyed the large garden—the three hundred strawberry plants with luscious fruit to pick for our desserts. Strawberry and ice cream was always a treat. We also had apple trees, peach trees, and apricot trees. Eating out of the garden kept us busy as well.

One weekend, Paul and I decided to visit my brother Harry and his wife, Ilene, in Prescott, as they wanted us to go up to the Blue Mountains, where they had a cabin. It was a wonderful weekend where I had a chance to ride a snowmobile by myself—what an experience! While we visited, Harry mentioned they had a piece of property for sale in Long Beach, Washington, only a few blocks from the ocean. I looked at Paul for approval and said, "It is sold." Paul nodded his approval! I said, "I cannot handle the dust anymore in George."

Even though there was much to do in George—the Fourth of July celebrations, the great celebrations on Washington's birthday, friendships of Mayor and Mrs. Brown and the church family—it was best to go to an area where I did not have carry the Kleenex box with me at all times.

Praise God and the grace and mercy of God to take us out of the dust bowl.

# Move to Long Beach

Oh, the fresh air greeted us as we drove into Long Beach; the breeze from the Pacific Ocean was gently engulfing us as we drove down the main street, where there was much activity going on. The merry-go-round was full of vacationers, and as we looked out toward the ocean, it was loaded with people laughing and flying kites. Oh, what an atmosphere to come into!

We were so pleased with our lot. Behind us was a lake, and a creek ran alongside our property. It was up a bit, so we would have good drainage of water from our mobile home. I was delighted, and so was Paul. Oh, how we thanked God for this piece of property for us to enjoy and relax!

Harry and Ilene came over as often as they could from Prescott to take us out on their boat to go fishing for salmon. I loved to fish, but one time we went out about ten miles off the Long Beach coastline, and two times I caught a shark. No, thanks. When I reeled him in and I saw that big mouth of his, Ilene cut my line, and again, I cast out my line and caught another shark. That was my last time fishing for salmon; I would buy mine from the fish market, as there were several fish markets to buy the fish.

Each weekday, we would go to the senior center for lunch just to get out of the house. Paul always wanted to take a break from work, and, of course, I loved to do different things in the area. We had good neighbors whom we could visit with and go to the Eagles, the Elks, and, of course, our church.

The first appearance at the closest Lutheran church to our home on the Long Beach Peninsula was in Chinook. I met my old friends from Seattle, Margaret and Roy Anderson, and the next Tuesday, I was in their Bible study in the home of Donna and Dave Oatfield. I met wonderful Christian people, Louise and Jackie, and many others who made up this wonderful Christian group.

Paul and I enjoyed going to the ocean to dig up razor clams. It was such fun to see thousands of people coming to do the same thing, just crowding in for their special spot to dig for clams. Oh, how they clamored for that clam. I saw one woman just open up one clam and eat it there on the spot. It nearly made me lose my stomach, and I thought to myself, *The clams should not be eaten raw but cooked through*. My first experience cooking them was disastrous. They were tough as nails, so I had to throw them out. Paul enjoyed digging for the clams, but eating them was a different matter.

We had a huge garden, brought over some oregano from the ranch, had many trees, a hot house, and did a lot of canning, to say nothing of the drying of foods, fruits, and vegetables.

In 1980, Kathi suggested we take a trip over to Hawaii for a couple of weeks so we could visit the grave of my brother Robert, who was killed in World War II on Saipan in 1944 while on duty in the Marine Corps. My brother's body was brought to Hawaii to be buried in the national cemetery there. Paul did not want to go because he did not want to fly, nor did he want to go by boat. Kathi and I had a wonderful trip. It was so nice to view the customs of Hawaii, their food, and the many sights.

In 1982, Paul and I decided to purchase a fifth wheel and start traveling. This gave Paul a tremendous freedom he needed, as he did a lot of work there on our property clearing off trees and debris from the area close to the lake. He loved going from place to place, and Harry and Ilene would travel with us. Paul and I decided one winter to go to Yuma, Arizona, and left Long Beach November 15, 1982. What a great time we had in Yuma! There was so much to do there—the square and round dancing, going to swap meets, and, our first priority, the Lutheran church! We met some of the most loving people there, and one of their members had an exercise class once a week in their fellowship hall. It was great!

Each winter, we would take trips into California, where we visited with our dear friends, the Bahadursinghs, Ardyce and Rai, in Sacramento and Paul's sister and brother-in-law, Mary and John Mauro, in Oakland, and their families, some in Hollywood. It was always a delight to see them.

It was not long before Helen and Jerry Watson moved into the mobile home that Harry and Ilene vacated. They were such energetic people. They loved to fish, and Helen did a lot of canning. They had a large garden to keep them busy, along with all the other things they had to do. What a great time we had visiting with each other, having coffee, and just enjoying each other!

My continued Bible study with Donna and her group became more relaxed, so one week I confessed my problem with the seizures. She, Donna, and Louise and the whole group anointed me with oil, and they prayed the Lord would heal me! And He did! What a relief that was! I can never thank and praise Him enough, even into eternity!

I had an MRI of my brain taken, and my brain turned out to be normal! Praise be to the Father! I have the papers in my purse stating the good results of the MRI. Oh God, You are so good—all we have to do is ask, if we would believe. Oh God, I love You so much I cannot tell You because I don't have the words to express my joy and happiness at Your wonderful love for me! All fear is gone!

# Paul's Misfortune

One day, I thought it would be nice to have some of our salmon for lunch. I always carefully look over the fish to remove any bones and cook it just right. Paul is careful to inspect the fish also, but one of the bones was overlooked, and Paul got one of the bones caught in his esophagus, much to our dismay.

We had a hospital just three miles from home, but we drove one hundred and ten miles to Group Health Hospital, where we were members, an HMO. We thought maybe it would be best to go to Olympia, as I could not imagine the expense involved.

When Paul was checked in, the doctor said he would feed Paul through the vein, as he had possibly lost a lot of fluid that needed to be replaced. Then came the shocker: Paul was to be given a medication to dissolve the fish bone, the doctor said. I questioned the doctor as to the strength of this pill. Would it be too strong? Was he able to tolerate the medication? The doctor said, "Paul is well able to tolerate the medication because he is healthy and strong."

I called the doctor after a couple of days and told him Paul's tongue was purple. The doctor said, "That is okay. Paul is healthy and strong, and he can tolerate the pills."

Who am I to distrust my doctor? I trusted my doctor, so I had no choice. This was about 1988, and I had a strong desire to go back to talk to the doctor, only to find out he was in Australia for one year. This was strange, I thought.

While we were in Olympia, I wanted Paul's heart to be checked because he was having chest pains. Sure enough, after the examination, Paul was given heart medication. Then before long, Paul complained. He had tumors removed from his intestines. Then he was sent to Longview to have an operation there in the hospital for an aneurysm two inches above the navel that led to his heart, then came the prostate problem, then his eyes had to have surgery, then I noticed he was a bit forgetful, though not too much at first.

Paul had determination. He did not want to give up driving, but he became easily irritated, so I had to be extra careful and considerate of his feelings, as I loved him for his struggles.

I could hardly wait for my doctor to get back to Olympia so I could confront him with Paul's health problems. I later found out he was no longer working at Group Health Hospital but was working at another hospital just down the street. What was Group Health Hospital covering up? I asked Group Health for the name of the pill they gave Paul, and they would not give it to me. Strange.

I have always been careful in keeping track of all our medications and vitamins, but for some strange reason, and I suppose the trauma I was under, the medication name and bottle was misplaced, much to my regret. Or maybe the Lord had His hand in this to keep me from pursuing legal actions against Group Health Hospital.

I have forgiven Group Health and their practices and what they did to my beloved husband, as well as the trauma he had to go through. And he has yet to come through it because of their lack of compassion and their concern for the almighty dollar. I even had to pay for the medication that ruined my husband's health. I have forgiven them for what they did, and I asked God to bless them. You see, I do not have the last word; only God does! I have asked God to take away the hurt they caused Paul and me and our family. Group Health Hospital has stolen years away from Paul and me and our family, and they will not have to answer to me but to God!

I can only conclude that what they gave Paul to dissolve the fish bone was some form of acid or dynamite. Paul has had several heart attacks and strokes since then, but he has stamina; praise God! All praise and thanks to You, Almighty God, for seeing us through this time of trial!

One day, Paul and I were on our way to Astoria for a day of relaxation when I mentioned that maybe we should stop by the home of "Gertrude," who had lost her husband and was a member of our church. (I will call her Gertrude to protect the innocent.) Each week, we would pick her up on our way to Astoria to have lunch at the Moose or some other place. She seemed lonesome, and she belonged to our church.

I noticed she would squeeze in between Paul and me when we would walk down the street, or when we were sitting down somewhere, she would sit between us, but to my horror, she could not keep her hands off Paul. I noticed, even at church (it did not make any difference where) or after church, while everyone was sitting around little tables, she would sit between us and put her hands on his knees under the table. I thought it was strange for Gertrude to do this. What is she trying to do? I wanted to talk to the pastor, but then I thought it was silly. Surely Gertrude did not mean anything by it. This kept on for some time, and each time, I grew a little more agitated at her behavior. Paul was not discouraging her from touching him, so I thought he was enjoying her attention.

This continued on for a while until I confronted Paul about Gertrude and her actions. Did he have feeling for her? I said, "Paul, I love you very much, but if you would rather have the attention of Gertrude, I will not hold you back; I will release you from our marriage." He did not say anything but went out to the garage to his workshop. A few minutes later, Kathi came to visit us and went out to say hello to her dad.

Before long, she came back, saying, "Dad is crying because you want a divorce."

I dashed out to see him and told him I didn't want a divorce but maybe he did.

He said, "Absolutely not. I don't want a divorce, and I have no feelings for Gertrude." I am so glad he said no!

Oh, how happy I was; my happiness was restored. Thank You, precious Father, for having Kathi come and get down to the bottom of our situation with Gertrude. Needless to say, the next time I saw Gertrude, I told her to keep her hands off my husband and don't forget it.

Paul has been so good to me, I cannot think of a harsh word he ever said to me, nor did he say no to anything, except once before we were married when I wanted to give his engagement ring back because I did not want him to be married to a woman with my illness. He said, "Absolutely no," and again said no to a divorce because of Gertrude. Oh, praise God for this wonderful, loving husband of mine. I will always love and cherish him. To God be the glory.

Our precious great-granddaughter, Lydia Pacific LaLonde, born March 12, 1998, to Casi and Gary LaLonde, was the pride of our life. She came to visit us for a few days when she was about two years old. She was such a joy to have with us. We had celebrated her second birthday, and it was summer, a time to go out to the ocean to watch the kites the people were flying, much to everyone's delight. She loved visiting with her beloved Pappa and Nana and Auntie Toni. Her understanding was far beyond her years. She brightened up our lives with her happy spirit.

One day, while she was with us, she saw her precious Pappa engulfed in flames—something she will never forget. While she was screaming, Toni and I were fighting the flames with a vengeance. Paul had reached across the stove for a knife that was on the wall when his nylon jacket accidently touched the hot burner; he was helping us fix breakfast. He was instantly engulfed in flames, and every second the fire became more intense. I was just a few feet from him when this happened, and I immediately threw water on him, but this made no difference. Then I hurriedly tore off his upper clothing and then told him to lie down on the rug while I smothered the flames with a throw rug. Paul had such a frightened look on his face while I tried to comfort him, saying, "Everything is okay. You are fine, and the fire is out."

Meanwhile, Toni was stepping on the flaming clothes I had torn off Paul and then tried to comfort little Lydia, who was still screaming, "Pappa is burning." I quickly called 911, and in minutes, the ambulance was there! Praise God! They took over and then put him in the ambulance and headed for the hospital.

I quickly gathered little Lydia and Toni and headed for the hospital. Paul received first- and second-degree burns on his right side, just below the armpit. I called the family and Casi, who then came down to Long Beach and took little Lydia home. Little Lydia was oh-so happy to see her mom and dad, as she was still so frightened, and I did not have the time to adequately comfort her.

Oh God, thank You for hearing my prayer as I was helping my beloved Paul. How thankful we were for You to come to our rescue when we need it so badly. It could have been disastrous had You not helped us!

Paul always talked to me about being careful and the benefits of safety, so this was a horrible experience not only for Paul but for all of us. I am positive in my spirit that Paul would have been more alert and careful had he not been through those horrible experiences of the past couple of years.

Thank You, precious Jesus, again and again for saving my beloved husband from disaster! Amen and amen!

# Desert Hot Springs

It was time to think about heading south again. The canning from the garden vegetables was put away for the winter. Paul had put his riding lawn mower away too for the winter. Saying to the neighbors, "See you later," and to our precious church family, saying, "See you in the spring," always brought a smile, but saying our good-byes to Pastor and Mrs. Bauder always choked us up.

We had sold our first fifth wheel, and then we purchased a smaller but more comfortable one. Paul always took such pride in getting his pick-up and fifth wheel ready for travel; they were in excellent condition and shining as only he could do!

Toni had retired from the Lighthouse for the Blind in Seattle in 1998 and was ready to come with us. She slept on the comfortable davenport. We stopped at our dear friends', the Bahadursinghses', then headed to visit Paul's relatives, then south to Desert Pools, where we had a membership. After a few weeks' stay there, we went to Catalina Spa. It was nice at Catalina Spa, as there seemed to be a more active program and we felt more at home there.

Catalina Spa had an active church program headed by Archie and LaVerne Phelps. It was an inspiring place and had the Catalina Spa Band, various programs during the week, and wonderful potlucks, with people from all over the United States and Canada joining in on all the activities.

We were smitten with Catalina and its programs. We thought, for our future, we should purchase a ten-year lease, so late winter, March 26, 1999, we signed the papers for one of the nicest things we have done. It was nice getting reacquainted with friends from the last season we had met in the Desert Hot Springs area visiting the Indio area, where one could experience many activities and where we could purchase fresh fruit at a real bargain.

We returned home to Long Beach, but I noticed Paul was having a bit of difficulty driving. I vowed the next time we went south, our family, especially Kathi and Lance, could help him. Oh, how thankful it was to safely reach home. Praise God for helping Paul! My heart went out to Paul, for he had always been there when we needed him, and I grieved for him and his efforts. Oh God, bless him immeasurably!

Toni bought a trailer in Ocean Park, Washington, from Ron Huber, the program's winter chairman of

Catalina Spa. Ron did some work at Catalina Spa, so he offered to bring the trailer south to Catalina for Toni. Praise God! What a help!

Kathi and Lance brought us down in their van. We left November 17, 1999, and arrived November 18, 1999, and left for Corona to purchase a Cavco park model on November 19, 1999. We had made inquiries ahead of time, so everything worked out just fine. Praise God! We loved the park model—it had a high ceiling, and Paul loved it and was proud of it. He seemed comfortable getting adjusted to it.

When we were ready to leave Desert Hot Springs, Kathi and Lance brought us home to Long Beach, and the first thing I did was had Paul checked out by the doctor so I could be alerted if a problem was to arise with him in the near future. He had a good doctor in Ilwaco at the medical center. The doctor gave me medications to give him, and I carefully carried them out and saw to it he had plenty of rest. He did not do much of anything at Long Beach but enjoyed the family and friends who stopped by to say hello and wished him well. Pastor Bauder stopped by, giving him prayer and encouragement. We visited the senior center often and went to church.

Kathi and Lance were eager to drive us down to Desert Hot Springs, and this was a much-needed help. We found everything in good condition and, of course, welcomed the warmer weather. It was wonderful when Casi and her family came down for Thanksgiving. Little Lydia enjoyed the different programs and the swimming pool. We were alone for Christmas, but the greeting from family was enough to see us through the holidays! The many activities, at that time of the year, were just exploding in the park, and that kept us from being too lonesome for the family.

On February 11, 2000, we had a huge porch built alongside our park model. Earlier, we had a shed put up on the back of our property, and Toni also had put up a shed for storage. Toni traded her trailer for a new champion fifth wheel. It was larger and more spacious. Then later we added a porch. Toni loves to line dance, and she needs the exercise because of her diabetes. I had to give up the line dancing and other activities so I could be with my beloved Paul and watch him closely. I was so concerned about him; I did not go out for walks and leave him home alone. We did go out for a breath of fresh air each day to get him out of the house, but these walks were slow and easy. There were nine trips to the emergency room from December 2000 to November 2002. He still noticed our friends and joked with them.

Our Catalina Bible study group and church group were invited to a once-a-month luncheon at Home Town Buffet, so Paul and I decided to go. This was March 8, 2002, and our friend Cliff Johnson took our picture. It was one of the best pictures I have ever seen taken of Paul. Oh, how I thanked Cliff for taking that picture! It was the last good picture I have of Paul. Paul's expression was as good as I have ever seen of him. So many times before when his picture was taken, his health problems were visible.

Paul was so happy to be with me, and that made me feel so good, and I was overjoyed! We remained in Desert Hot Springs for the summer and had to make severe adjustments because of the heat. This was such a contrast from what we were used to at Long Beach, where we had cool breezes coming off the Pacific Ocean. We had a swamp cooler put in the front window of the park model, but it was not satisfactory, so we had to put in an air conditioning system only after I heard my pastor say it was 127 degrees at 8:00 a.m. one Sunday morning at church. Oh, the air conditioning system worked beautifully! It was so nice to get out of the intense heat. We would get up early in the morning to do our shopping and then hurry home to our air conditioned home. Praise You, Jesus!

John and Millie Heidi, from the Catalina Spa, were super people in support of helping me with Paul. John was one of the security guards at the RV Park. John was a saint in helping me, and I don't know what I would have done had he not helped me. I rapidly became tired because of lack of sleep because I was always so busy taking care of Paul. John would take Paul out for a few hours so I could get some rest. "Oh God, please continue to bless John in every way," I prayed. "He has diabetes and had problems with his foot. Praise God; he seems to be doing okay! His wife is in a wheelchair, so she has my prayers too!"

Now dear Lord, I have come to the time when Paul had his heart attack (November 15, 2002) and Dr. Williams suggested Paul go to a nursing home. The doctor chose Manor Care, and Paul entered the home (November 21, 2002). This was covered in the first chapter of my story.

The story continues. The people at Manor Care are super people and are devoted to their work; Rochelle and Leilane and others have gone the extra mile in caring for Paul. I had a feeling I must go to visit Paul. It was as if I were driven to see him. I could not stay away because of my love for him. I was getting so tired, and Toni wanted to help me drive, but she could not because of her sight. I kept eating sugar to keep up my energy, and I know that was wrong, but I had to keep going. My doctor encouraged me to go on a vacation for a while and rest up. Toni and I had a chance to go on a boat trip on the *Millennium*. This was the boat's maiden voyage coming from San Diego through the Panama Canal, then up to Florida, but making stops along the way at Acapulco, Mexico, Cabo San Lucas, Mexico, Huatulco, Mexico, Oranjestad, Aruba, Panama Canal, Cruising Canal, Punternas, Costa Rico, and arriving in North Hollywood, Florida. I did not want to go because I would be leaving Paul, but the doctor said I should go, and I reluctantly went. While I was gone, I made several phone calls about Paul's situation, and they informed me, "All is well."

What a beautiful trip we had. The sights were breathtaking, the food was excellent and was served twenty-four hours a day, the weather was good—we only had rough water for a couple of days but not so rough that we could not stand on the deck of the ship. Each day, I could walk outside on the deck for the tremendous view, seeing other giant ships passing by and, of course, waving to them as if I knew them. Ships from other countries and passing through the fantastic Panama Canal is something I will never forget—the little cars going up and down on either side of the canal helping boats as they inched through the narrow canal. Then when we arrived in Florida, we were given a trip up through the Everglades.

This was interesting, but my heart was at home with Paul and worrying about him. I was anxious to get home and see him, and when I got there, he was scratching himself fiercely, saying, "I itch, I itch," and the look on his face was so anxious. Right then and there, I vowed I would never leave him again for any length of time. I saw to it that would never happen again to Paul.

I was still intensely driven to see Paul as often as I could, but I was tiring. Again, I started to eat more sweets to keep me going.

Toni had to leave for her class reunion in Vancouver, Washington. I became exhausted and had to go to the hospital because I had pneumonia, and my blood sugar was two hundred and twenty-five, and I felt utterly wiped out. Dr. Williams said I could have died. Only God saved me from this, as I was sorely needed by my darling Paul and Toni. I could only stay in the hospital three days, as I had to get home to help Toni get ready for her trip. Oh, how I thank Pat, a friend and office worker of the RV Park, for taking Toni to the airport.

The next day, Kathi's children, Casi and Pooter (also known as Vance Shaw), showed up to help me! Oh God, thank You for sending them down to help me, and I can never thank You enough! What a welcome they were! In the meantime, I was taking my medicine to recover from my illness, and I rested as much as I could. Casi and Pooter saw to it that I did. Then they drove me over to see their beloved grandpa. They stayed for a few days and then had to reluctantly leave to go home so they could go to work. Oh, how wonderful it was to have them here.

After about two weeks, Toni came home. Oh, what a relief it was to have her home. Her face was so drawn with worry, but when she saw I was better, she lost her worry lines. Praise God! Oh, the people at the park were so good to me by stopping by to visit and to help me. Even Steven Pendergast, the manager, stopped by. Others, such as Judy and Jerry Ruggeric, were always ready to take us where we needed to go.

It was getting almost impossible for me to drive often to see Paul, so frequent trips had to be cut back, but that terrified look on Paul's face drove me on to see him. Of course, this was the look I saw on his face after I returned from my boat trip.

Sometimes others would take me to see him, especially wonderful friends from the park, Leta and Ben Benefiel. Oh, what marvelous people they were to help.

They also drove Toni and me over to Los Angeles to the eye clinic, the Jules Stein Eye Institute at UCLA, so Toni could be tested for eye surgery. This was done three times in several months, and each time they said they could not operate.

We started to go to the Lyons Club in Desert Hot Springs. This was a tremendous blessing, as they recommended Toni see a Dr. VanDeuson, and he sent her to see Dr. Christopher Blanton. Oh, praise the Lord. He said after he had examined her eyes, "Yes, I can operate on her eyes!" Thank You, Jesus! Her operation turned out well! All thanks to You, Jesus!

# Desert Hot Springs Baptism

It seemed to me I could not get rid of the nervous feeling in my stomach—this feeling I have had for a long time since Paul entered Manor Care.

Then a miracle happened to me. I was asked to witness a water baptism, and I was eager to be present. I had always wanted to be water baptized since a friend of mine, Louise Nelson from Long Beach, Washington, had gone to and was water baptized in the Jordan River. She was so elated at having done so, and this had made a great impression on me. Yes, my parents had me baptized when I was an infant, but that was their decision, not mine. I wanted to be water baptized because it was my decision.

So December 21, 2003, just thirteen months after Paul entered Manor Care, Jack Marshall, a minister of the gospel and a participant at Catalina Spa Park

Church Services, with Archie Phelps, baptized Pauline Elliott and then asked me if I wanted to be baptized. "Of course," I said to Jack, "I have always wanted to be baptized in water…Yes!" I was not clothed for the baptism, but I said, "Let us go for it."

There are not enough words that can express the love I felt for the Lord as I came up out of the water. The shakiness, the nervousness, the apprehension were *gone*, and I was as cool as a cucumber! Calmness came over me, and I worshiped the Lord for His goodness to me! To this very day, I still thank and praise the Lord for the wonderful peace that replaced all of my anxiety! Thank You, blessed Jesus, for the miraculous healing You gave me! I felt the Holy Spirit working in me! There was a calm I did not think I could contain!

December 24, 2003, I found these scriptures:

> The Lord your God is with you. He is mighty to save. He will rejoice over you with song. He will delight in you. He will quiet you with His love.
> Zephaniah 3:17 (KJV)

> The Lord is faithful, He will strengthen you, and protect you from the evil one.
> 2 Thessalonians 3:3 (KJV)

> No weapon that is formed against you shall prosper, and every tongue that shall rise against you in judgment, Thou shalt condemn.
> Isaiah 54:17 (KJV)

For God has not given us a spirit of fear but of power and love and a calm and well-balanced mind and discipline and self control.
2 Timothy 1:7 (KJV)

Seven times a day do I praise thee because of thy righteous laws. Great peace have they which love thy law: and nothing shall offend them.
Psalm 119:164-165 (KJV)

# Sixty-Fourth Wedding Anniversary Revelation

I have done all that I can for my beloved Paul; in the name of the Father, Son, and Holy Spirit, I have done my best for him. Now I am placing and accepting Paul's health problem into the loving hands of the almighty God. Paul's health problem is out of my hands now and into the precious hands of the Lord! Paul is in a good facility with Rocelle, Leilane, Eleanor, Dome, Rose, and others. God bless all who care for him, yes, doctors and all.

I have asked God for help, and it came to me to surrender to the peace of God. Out of all this came a peace I have never known since Paul accidentally swallowed a fish bone and Group Health Hospital gave Paul a medication to dissolve the fish bone, only to cause Paul tremendous health problems. The devil has tried his best to discourage me. No more, Satan. You are a liar and the father of lies.

My main problem is to do all I can to let Paul know he is loved and wanted, to make him comfortable, to make him more aware of me. Now with my acceptance of his situation, anger, stress, anxiety, worry, etc., are gone! Now I have placed Paul into the loving hands of God—the *best* place Paul can be. I thank God for the sixty-five years of marriage to Paul and his tremendous love for me and my undying love and joy for our beloved family together. I do not want to have a feeling of negligence and guilt by letting him know how much he means to me.

Thank You, Jesus. You took all our pain and suffering on the cross for us, and there was a time when you were separated from Your Father for a time when You were on the cross. And later You went to be with Your Father, praise God, and came back on the third day! So now I have placed my beloved Paul into your loving care, knowing the best is yet to come. I thank You into eternity! Hallelujah!